Tong

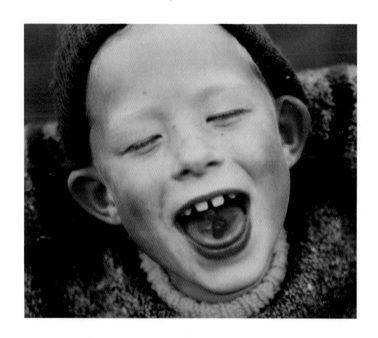

MW01043451

Written by Jo Windsor

Rigby

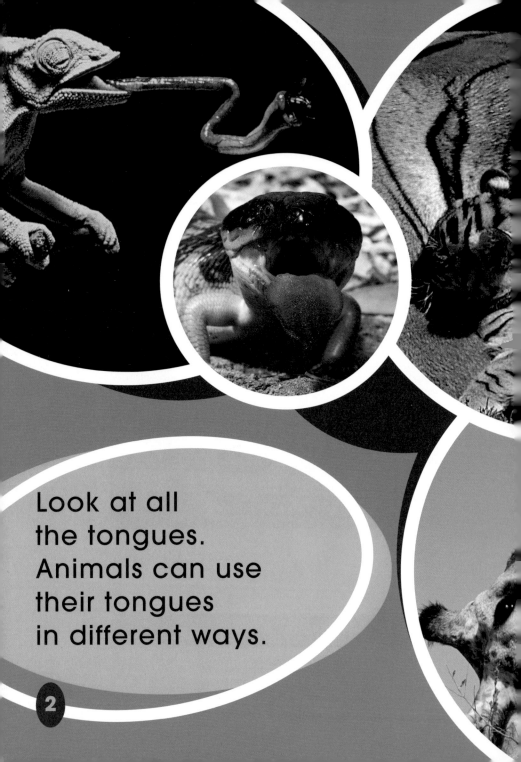

Look at all
the tongues.
Animals can use
their tongues
in different ways.

2

taste buds

Tongues can help us taste food.
They have little bumps on them.
The bumps are called taste buds.

4

tongue

Some animals use their
tongues to eat food.
This toad can flick out
its tongue to catch a fly.

tongue

Some animals
have sticky tongues.
This animal likes to
eat ants.
It uses its tongue
to get the ants.

ant

This animal likes
to eat ants, too.
It has a very long tongue.
It can get lots and lots
of ants with its tongue.

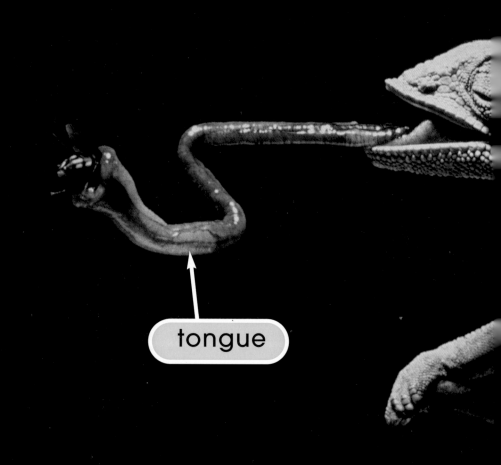

tongue

This animal has
a long tongue, too.
It can flick out its tongue
to catch a fly.

Some animals poke out
their tongues when
there is danger.
Look at this tongue.
It is red.

This animal has
a blue tongue.
When there is danger,
it can poke out its
blue tongue and hiss!

Some animals use their
tongues for cleaning.
This mother tiger
is cleaning her baby
with her tongue.

This whale has a
very big tongue.
It has the biggest tongue
in the world!

Index

Guide Notes

Title: Tongues
Stage: Early (4) – Green

Genre: Nonfiction (Expository)
Approach: Guided Reading
Processes: Thinking Critically, Exploring Language, Processing Information
Written and Visual Focus: Photographs (static images), Labels, Index

THINKING CRITICALLY
(sample questions)
- Look at the title and read it to the children. Ask: "What do you think this book is going to tell us?"
- Ask the children what they know about tongues.
- Focus the children's attention on the Index. Ask: "What are you going to find out about in this book?"
- If you want to find out about a sticky tongue, on which page would you look?
- If you want to find out about a long tongue, on which pages would you look?
- Look at pages 6 and 7. What is the difference between the tongues of these animals?
- Look at pages 7 and 8. Why do you think having a long tongue can help these animals?
- Look at pages 12 and 13. What might the mother tiger's tongue be like to help her clean her baby?

EXPLORING LANGUAGE

Terminology
Title, cover, photographs, author, photographers

Vocabulary
Interest words: flick, tongue, sticky, danger, hiss
High-frequency word (new): use
Positional word: out

Print Conventions
Capital letter for sentence beginnings, periods, commas, exclamation mark